South Slammers
The Final Years

MARK V. PIKE

BRITAIN'S RAILWAYS SERIES, VOLUME 64

Front cover image: This is Vauxhall station, about two miles out of London Waterloo, as Class 412 4-CEP 2313 heads west with a train for Portsmouth. Unfortunately, this once fine view, with Big Ben and the Houses of Parliament in the background has now been obliterated by tree growth. The unit itself was withdrawn in October 2004. 24 October 2003.

Title page image: Arriving at Brockenhurst for their naming ceremony and entry into traffic from Bournemouth Depot are immaculate 3-CIG pair 1497+1498, both with covered nameplates. The pair had to run into the main up platform to be able to gain access to the down loop via a crossover at the western end of the station. 12 May 2005.

Back cover image: Viewed from the High Street footbridge at Poole, this is Class 412 4-CEP 2311 approaching the station with a terminating service. The line here is reversible from the crossing that the train has just used to swap from the down line to the up line and through the station. These trains often terminated on the up platform and still do, as it saves passengers with heavy luggage from having to cross the footbridge at the station. 26 May 2004.

Published by Key Books
An imprint of Key Publishing Ltd
PO Box 100
Stamford
Lincs PE9 1XQ

www.keypublishing.com

The right of Mark V. Pike to be identified as the author of this book has been asserted in accordance with the Copyright, Designs and Patents Act 1988 Sections 77 and 78.

Copyright © Mark V. Pike, 2025

ISBN 978 1 80282 828 3

All rights reserved. Reproduction in whole or in part in any form whatsoever or by any means is strictly prohibited without the prior permission of the Publisher.

Typeset by SJmagic DESIGN SERVICES, India.

Contents

Introduction 3

Chapter 1   Main Lines – South and East 4

Chapter 2   Lymington Branch (The Heritage Line) 53

Chapter 3   Loco Hauled/Propelled 72

Introduction

What became retrospectively known as 'slam-door trains' were the norm on the British system ever since the railways began, and appeared on almost all types. On the Southern Region, electric multiple-units (EMUs), also with slam doors, came into being after some lines were electrified in the 1930s, and remained in service until replaced in the 1950s and 1960s with similar new units. The first of these were high-density commuter units for working the suburban lines around the capital, but a little later, more comfortable longer-distance trains came on stream, some converted from existing loco-hauled stock of the period. Many examples from this generation provided sterling service all the way up to the mid-2000s. Among them were those that received codes such as 4-REP, 4-CEP and 4-VEP.

Enthusiasts often chase any form of well-known locos/units that are about to be withdrawn and these EMUs, latterly known generically as 'slammers' rather than by their class number, were no exception in their final years, as they gradually gave way to new units featuring automatic doors.

Viewed from the signal box, BR blue 4-VEP 3417 *Gordon Pettitt* approaches Harmans Cross on a Norden to Swanage service, propelled by both 33111+33108. It is showing headcode 97 for the Lymington branch! 11 May 2013.

Chapter 1

Main Lines – South and East

Left: We start this pictorial selection at the well-known location of Eastleigh in Hampshire, which had been a hub of slam-door electric multiple-unit (EMU) activity for many years. This is Class 423 4-VEP 3812, leading another of the class on the eastern approach to the station with a southbound service for Portsmouth Harbour. This unit was withdrawn from service in March 2005. 5 August 2004.

Below: Almost at the same spot is Class 411 4-CEP 1553, heading away from the camera with a service for London Waterloo. This unit was withdrawn just three months after this shot was taken in May 2004. 5 February 2004.

Class 423 4-VEP 3810 became a minor celebrity towards the end of its days, as it was briefly used for test purposes in Germany during 2002 in preparation for the new Class 450/444 units then being developed. It was also the last example still in service in the base Network Southeast livery without the addition of the orange stripe associated with South West Trains (SWT). It is seen here on the rear of a Bournemouth to London Waterloo semi-fast service awaiting to depart. I believe there was a half-hearted attempt to preserve this unit but, unfortunately, it came to nothing and withdrawal ensued in March 2005 just a month after this shot was taken. 2 February 2005.

Slammers galore! Class 423 4-VEP 3456 is seen approaching the station with a London Waterloo to Portsmouth Harbour train, whilst Class 421 4-CIG 1881 heads in the opposite direction on the rear of a London Waterloo-bound service led by another unidentified 4-CIG. 3456 was withdrawn during December 2004, and 1881 succumbed in May 2005. 1 July 2004.

Viewed from the vantage point of Campbell Road Bridge, Class 412 4-CEP 2315 leads a London Waterloo to Poole semi-fast service, having just called at Eastleigh. This was the final example of this class to remain in service, being withdrawn just two months after this shot was taken. However, it has been preserved many miles from its original working area, on the Eden Valley Railway in Cumbria. There is no third rail here, but the unit is occasionally used simply as loco-hauled coaching stock. 24 January 2005.

Now moving further east to the capital, we are at Vauxhall station, about two miles out of London Waterloo as Class 412 4-CEP 2313 heads west with a train for Portsmouth. Unfortunately, this fine view with Big Ben and the Houses of Parliament in the background has now been obliterated by tree growth. The unit itself was withdrawn in October 2004. 24 October 2003.

Looking in the opposite direction at Vauxhall, we see a thoroughly battered-looking Class 411 4-CEP, 1555, passing through with an Alton to London Waterloo train. This unit was withdrawn in July 2004. 24 October 2003.

Right: We are now at Tonbridge station in Kent, where Class 423 4-VEP 3573 is awaiting departure with a Hastings to Charing Cross service. This unit was withdrawn from service in June 2005. 13 November 2003.

Below: Heading east through Tonbridge station is Class 423 4-VEP 3585, leading a 12-coach formation as an empty stock move to an unknown destination. This unit was withdrawn in July 2005. 13 November 2003.

In full Connex livery, a Charing Cross to Hastings service calls at Tonbridge station with Class 423 4-VEP 3422 trailing. The station here is always recognisable by the bridge in the background with the unusually shaped arches. This unit was withdrawn in December 2004. 13 November 2003.

Up until about 2003/04, South Eastern-based units regularly worked as far west as Bournemouth on services from Gatwick Airport/Brighton (via the 'Coastaway' line). After this point in time, the service was curtailed to Southampton, using new Class 377 units that still run today. This is Class 421 4-CIG 1850 in the heart of the New Forest National Park, just south of Beaulieu Road station with a Bournemouth to Gatwick Airport service. Forest is the operative word here! At this time, lineside tree growth reached epic proportions and much of it was later cut back, but 23 years on, in 2024, it has all returned. This unit was among the last examples withdrawn during November 2005. 22 September 2001.

A 20-minute or so walk from the previous location, we see Class 421 4-CIG 1707 approaching Beaulieu Road from the opposite direction with a Gatwick Airport to Bournemouth service. Since this shot was taken, lineside tree growth has once again become overwhelming here and it is now difficult even to see the line. This unit was withdrawn in February 2005. 22 September 2001.

Returning to Eastleigh and this is Class 421 'Greyhound' 4-CIG 1322 drawing to a halt with a London Waterloo to Portsmouth service. The nickname 'Greyhound' was coined for these units in the number range 1301–1322 and 1392–1399 due to various modifications being added to increase performance and reliability, which included enhanced acceleration. This unit was one of the later SWT examples to go, ending its service during May 2005. 13 May 2004.

Above: Led by a pair of Class 423 4-VEP units, this is Class 421 4-CIG 1881 bringing up the rear of a Poole to London Waterloo train on its way out of Eastleigh. 1881 was another of the last units in service for SWT, and was withdrawn in May 2005. 1 July 2004.

Left: Just after a winter shower, Class 421 'Greyhound' 4-CIG 1309 is at Southampton Central, ready to depart with an all-stations stopping service to Portsmouth Harbour. These services are now in the hands of South Western Railway (SWR) Class 450 'Desiro' units. 1309 was also withdrawn in May 2005. 14 January 2004.

Just to the right of the train in the last shot, but on a different date, is South Eastern Class 421 4-CIG 1708, waiting to depart with a Bournemouth to Brighton/Gatwick Airport train. These trains are now worked by Southern-operated Class 377 units. 1708 was withdrawn in February 2005. 3 December 2003.

Above: The down bay (platform 5) at Southampton Central has not seen passengers for many years, but is occasionally used for stabling units and locos, although this practice has decreased in recent years. This is Class 411 4-CEP 1573 in the bay, either acting as a spare, or possibly due to a failure. It was withdrawn in April 2004, just three months after this shot was taken. 13 January 2004.

Right: Back to the South East again, where Class 421 4-CIG 1834 is captured leading an unidentified southbound service towards Horley, a mile or so north of Gatwick Airport. This unit was one of the last to be withdrawn from service in November 2005. 11 February 2004.

This is Class 423 4-VEP 3530 heading away from the camera at Horley to its next stop at Gatwick Airport. Along with unit 3486, this was to become the last Class 423 to move under its own power on the national network when on 15 December 2005 the pair worked from Brighton Lovers Walk Depot to Stewarts Lane Depot as an empty coaching stock (ECS) move. 11 February 2004.

With light sparking from the third rail, Class 423 4-VEP 3437 passes through Horley on the rear of a southbound service. This unit was withdrawn from service during December 2004. 11 February 2004.

Also departing from Horley is Class 423 4-VEP 3523, this time on the rear of a southbound stopping service. In the distance through the haze, Gatwick Airport station can just be discerned. This unit was withdrawn in June 2005 after a typically uneventful life. 11 February 2004.

Back on the South Western Division again and this is Class 412 4-CEP 2317 arriving at Bournemouth with a Wareham to Brockenhurst stopping service. The wide space between the platforms here reflects that there were once two middle roads through the station prior to the rationalisation and electrification of 1967. Also, beyond the ugly concrete flyover that was built in the 1970s, there was a steam depot that had a large allocation of locos, and was one of the last in operation right up to the end of steam workings on the Southern Region. 2317 was withdrawn at the end of September 2004, a couple of months after this shot. 23 July 2004.

Under the superb overall roof at Bournemouth is Class 421 4-CIG 1884 with a Brockenhurst to Wareham stopping service. During the late 1990s, the roof of this station became very unstable and something needed to be done as the potential for a serious accident was high, especially when there were strong winds that often blew out some of the glass panels that remained. It was for this reason that it was totally refurbished in the early 2000s and remains in excellent condition to this day. The unit was withdrawn in February 2005, just a couple of weeks after it was photographed here. 25 January 2005.

Just to the east of Bournemouth station, there is a short tunnel that passes beneath Holdenhurst Road, and it is from its eastern entrance that we see Class 423 4-VEP 3569 approaching with another Brockenhurst to Wareham stopping service. To the right of this image, where the coaches are parked up is the site of the original station of Bournemouth East, which was a terminus, on what was basically a branch line from Brockenhurst. It only had a life of 15 years or so, and was closed when today's station was brought into use in 1885 to accompany the extension of the line. Photos of the original station are just about non-existent, as is this unit which was withdrawn in April 2005. 9 March 2005.

A significant bit of railway history. Soon after arrival at Bournemouth, complete with the 'Lymington Flyer' headboard, Class 421 4-CIG 'Greyhound' units 1396+1398 are seen with the 11.35 London Waterloo to Bournemouth train, SWT's final public timetabled (non-railtour) working. The two units forming this train then proceeded forward empty stock to Bournemouth Depot and were withdrawn from service. 26 May 2005.

Here is Class 411 4-CEP 1699, arriving at Eastleigh with a service from Portsmouth to London Waterloo. This unit, along with 1697/98, was withdrawn by SWT during May 2004 but instead of being scrapped, they were transferred to the South Eastern Division and saw about a further year's work, later becoming the last 4-CEP units in normal service. 1699 was finally withdrawn from service in July 2005. 23 December 2003.

This is Class 423 4-VEP 3535 coming out of Eastleigh Works and heading back East. I think some Eastern-based units visited the works for attention around this time, but it was quite unusual for these to be seen at this location. The unit was withdrawn in December 2005. 13 May 2004.

We are now at Barnham, West Sussex, where Class 421 4-COP 1410 is departing with a service bound for Bognor Regis. This was previously a 3-car unit that had been reformed with the addition of an extra coach. The fine old signal box to the right was closed at the end of 2008; however, it has been preserved nearby and, despite a senseless arson attack that almost destroyed it completely, I believe it has now been fully restored and is on show to the public. The same cannot be said of the unit, which was withdrawn from service in March 2005. 3 December 2003.

Barnham signal box is seen again in this shot as Class 423 4-VOP 3907 arrives with an eastbound service on that same gloomy winter day. This unit was withdrawn in March 2005. 3 December 2003.

The location now is Purley, where Class 423 4-VEP 3515 leads a London Victoria-bound service towards the station. This unit was withdrawn in August 2004. 11 February 2004.

Still at Purley, this is Class 421 4-CIG 1803, calling with an unidentified southbound service. Purley will probably be remembered for all the wrong reasons, due to the March 1989 train crash there that claimed the lives of eight people. 1803 was withdrawn in July 2004. 11 February 2004.

This is the rarely photographed up loop platform at Brockenhurst as Class 412 4-CEP 2311 arrives with a terminating stopping service from Wareham. For obvious reasons, the preservation of any of these electric units relies on the presence of an electrified third rail to provide power and, to date, no heritage lines in the UK have this facility and are not really likely to. However, this does not prevent units being hauled by a diesel loco. This is precisely what preservationists have done with this unit and 2315 mentioned earlier. With just a few modifications, they can now be used as loco-hauled coaching stock on the Eden Valley Railway, Cumbria, as required. 3 October 2004.

Class 423 4-VEP 3405 is departing from the same loop at Brockenhurst that we saw in the previous shot, from the western end with a Brockenhurst to Wareham all-stations stopper. This unit was withdrawn in April 2005. 2 September 2004.

About a mile or so further west from Brockenhurst is (or rather was) Lymington Junction, where we see Class 423 4-VEP 3467 leading a 12-coach formation on a London Waterloo to Poole semi-fast service. The junction itself used to be just behind where I was standing, but since the mid-1970s, the single line to Lymington has been separate from the main line between here and Brockenhurst station; see also the next shot. This unit was withdrawn just a month after this shot was taken in February 2005. 8 January 2005.

Class 421 4-CIG 1881 passes the former Lymington Junction, leading another 12-coach formation on a Poole to London Waterloo service. The electrical substation just glimpsed to the left marks almost exactly where the old junction signal box used to stand, and opposite this to the right of the train was the junction of the original line that went via Ringwood and Wimborne to Hamworthy, prior to the construction of the more direct line via Christchurch to Bournemouth and Poole. The 'old road', as it was often referred to, was closed in 1964. 1881 was withdrawn from service in April 2005. 8 January 2005.

Deep in the heart of the New Forest National Park, Class 423 4-VEP 3433 leads another 12-car formation just south of Beaulieu Road station with a London Waterloo to Poole semi-fast service. Unfortunately, this fine view has now become ridiculously overgrown with trees and bushes. This unit succumbed to withdrawal in August 2004. 17 January 2004.

Class 421 4-CIG 'Greyhound' unit 1313 is seen departing from Eastleigh with a London Waterloo to Portsmouth stopping service. Withdrawal for this unit came in December 2004. 25 March 2004.

Left: Also departing Eastleigh is Class 423 4-VEP 3578, leading another 4-VEP on a London Waterloo to Poole semi-fast service. This unit was withdrawn in August 2004. 20 August 2003.

Below: Just about to make the Eastleigh stop is Class 421 4-CIG 'Greyhound' 1307 with a stopping service for London Waterloo. It is interesting to note the two differing shades of blue on these two units. This example was withdrawn in October 2004. 20 July 2004.

Above: Leading a 12-car 4-CIG formation towards Campbell Road at Eastleigh is 'Greyhound' 1397 with a Poole to London Waterloo train. This unit was withdrawn just three weeks after this shot, during May 2005. 20 April 2005.

Right: Around five miles south of Eastleigh is St Denys, where the line to Portsmouth meets the main London to Southampton and Weymouth line. Pulling away from the station with a Portsmouth to Southampton Central stopping train is Class 411 4-CEP 2311. This unit was withdrawn from service in April 2004, a month after this image was taken. 20 March 2004.

The line from St Denys to Portsmouth is also used by South Eastern-based trains, as it still is today with more modern Class 377s. This is Class 421 4-CIG 1908 at the same spot as the previous shot with a London Victoria to Southampton Central (via Worthing) service. The unit is painted in what was then the new South Central two-tone green and white livery. It was withdrawn in October 2004. 20 March 2004.

Class 423 4-VEPs were less common on these 'Coastaway' services, but this is 3501, approaching St Denys with a service eventually destined for London Victoria. This unit was withdrawn in December 2004. 20 March 2004.

Moving west of Southampton Central, Class 421 4-CIG 1884 is passing Millbrook (Hants) with a London Waterloo to Weymouth fast service. At the time, these workings were usually formed of Class 442 'Wessex Electrics', but 'slammers' did occasionally stand in. A shot from this position is now impossible, as the bridge has been curtailed to span just the one line (to the left of this shot) and serve the island platform and the adjacent road only. This unit was taken out of service in February 2005. 30 March 2004.

Still at Millbrook (Hants) but from the other end of the footbridge, this is Class 421 4-CIG 1884, passing through with a stopping service bound for Poole. This unit was removed from service in February 2005. 2 September 2004.

The footbridge from which the previous two shots were taken is seen in the background here as Class 423 4-VEP 3516 passes through eastbound with an empty stock working. Funnily enough, the left edge of this image denotes almost exactly where the bridge has now been chopped off. The same fate befell this unit when it was withdrawn in April 2005. 17 December 2004.

Now very much a 'celebrity', Class 423 4-VEP 3417 *Gordon Pettitt* was returned to all-over BR blue livery in early 2004 and was involved in many of the farewell specials run at the time. Since withdrawal from normal service in April 2005, it has mostly been in storage at various locations in the south of England, but has also been used behind many types of diesel locos on semi-regular visits to the Swanage Railway. As of early 2024, it is based at Strawberry Hill, and moves are currently in hand to get it main-line registered. The unit is seen here at the pleasant location of Holes Bay, just west of Poole, with a Wareham to Brockenhurst stopping service. 3 December 2004.

A couple of weeks later, 3417 was on the same circuit as in the previous shot, and is seen arriving here at Poole with a Brockenhurst to Wareham stopper. 17 December 2004.

After boarding the train at Poole, I was able to get this shot of 3417 soon after arriving at Wareham station. After passengers had alighted, the unit then usually moved back to the sidings behind the bridge I was standing on. 17 December 2004.

This is one of the farewell tours mentioned earlier. 4-VEP 3417 and Class 421 3-CIG 1497 are arriving at Bournemouth about 20 minutes late with 1Z81, the 09.02 London Waterloo to Weymouth 'Seaside Slammer' charter organised by South West Trains. A Class 442 'Wessex Electric' awaits departure for London Waterloo in the up platform. Details for 3-CIG 1497 can be found in the next section of this book. 18 June 2005.

Here is Class 423 4-VOP 3902 pulling away from Southampton Central after arriving with a service from London Victoria/Gatwick Airport. I believe the 4-VOPs were essentially 4-VEPs but with the first-class accommodation removed to provide more standard class seating. This unit was withdrawn from service in May 2005.

Above: Also at Southampton Central, on a day of sunshine and showers, this is Class 421 4-CIG 1868 arriving from the up sidings to form a Gatwick Airport/London Victoria train. This unit was also withdrawn from service during May 2005. 26 November 2003.

Left: This is another Class 421 4-CIG, 1712, arriving from the up sidings into Southampton Central to form another Gatwick Airport/London Victoria service. This unit was taken out of service in January 2005.

Class 421 4-CIG 1862 became the last of a handful of units to receive the South Central two-tone green and white livery, and is seen here negotiating the pointwork at the southern end of Southampton Central as it heads towards the up siding to stable. The unit was withdrawn from service in July 2005. 18 February 2004.

Moving south, we are now in the Poole area for a series of images. Viewed from the High Street footbridge, this is Class 412 4-CEP 2311 approaching the station with a terminating service. The line here is reversible from the crossing that the train has just used to swap from the down line to the up line and through the station. These terminating trains were (and still do) often terminate on the up platform, as it saves passengers with heavy luggage from having to cross the footbridge at the station. Rather surprisingly, even in 2024, Poole station does not have any lifts, just a small footbridge dating from the early 1970s. This unit has been preserved as detailed earlier in this volume. 26 May 2004.

This shot is taken from the Poole station footbridge mentioned in the previous caption. Class 412 4-CEP 2316 is arriving with another stopping service, this time from Wareham to Brockenhurst. The signal box that can just be made out to the top left of the picture was closed in 2014 and demolished soon after. This unit was taken out of service during September 2004. 31 March 2004.

Taken from what was then a relatively new Seldown Road bridge, Class 423 4-VEP 3810, the minor celebrity mentioned at the beginning of this section, is seen departing from Poole and passing the Wilts & Dorset bus station to the right. The High Street footbridge can be seen in the background, while the supermarket to the left is built on what was originally a huge gas-works site that was demolished in the mid-1970s. The unit also met a similar fate after being withdrawn just a month after this shot was taken in March 2005. 22 February 2005.

Taken from the same bridge as the previous view but looking in the opposite direction, is Class 412 4-CEP 2311 again, this time with a Brockenhurst to Wareham stopping service. It is difficult to believe that up until the early 1970s, when land reclamation took place, the housing estate in the background would have been in the sea! 20 January 2004.

Sister unit Class 412 4-CEP 2312 stands at Poole station with a Wareham to Brockenhurst stopping service. This unit was taken out of service in October 2004. 18 May 2004.

Right: It is not always sunny in Poole! On a miserable damp morning, this is Class 423 4-VEP 3520, departing with a Wareham to Brockenhurst stopping service. Note the spare rails dotted around between the platforms; this very sharp curve has always suffered with excessively worn rails and require regular monitoring for wear. This unit was withdrawn during April 2005. 15 October 2004.

Below: This is a view over the fence as Class 412 4-CEP 2316 is seen again, this time passing Baiter, about half a mile or so north of Poole, with another stopping train bound for Brockenhurst. 28 May 2004.

Half a mile further east than the previous shot, we see Class 421 4-CIG 'Greyhound' 1393 drifting down the 1-50 incline of Parkstone Bank with a Brockenhurst to Wareham stopper. Though not easily apparent from this angle, the train is passing over the very narrow bridge here; the passage underneath it is just about wide enough for one car at a time and has caused many a problem over the years for vehicles that have proved to be too wide or too tall! This unit has had a bit of a muddled time since withdrawal in April 2005. It was originally purchased for preservation by the Great Central Railway and restored to its as-built green livery and number 7059. However, various coaches were later sold on and used in main line test trains, but I am not sure if they still are in 2024. Some coaches were also scrapped. 1 February 2005.

Back to the South East now for a few shots as we see Class 423 4-VOP 3907 approaching a misty and cold Arundel with a stopping train for Littlehampton. This unit was withdrawn in March 2005. 3 December 2003.

The same service as the previous shot is making the call at Arundel as the weak winter sun tries its best to warm things up. 3 December 2003.

Here we see Class 423 4-VEP 3551 awaiting departure from Tonbridge with a service for London Bridge via Redhill. This unit was withdrawn from service in September 2004. 13 February 2004.

Class 421 4-CIG 1720 is in the loop platform at Worthing with an unidentified service for London. This unit was withdrawn in August 2004. 3 December 2003.

Now we head to the south-western extremity of the third-rail network on the South Coast at Weymouth, on a very wet day, where firstly we see Class 421 4-CIG 1394 'Greyhound' in platform 2 awaiting departure with a service for Poole/Bournemouth and eventually London Waterloo. Due to a defect on one of the coaches, this unit was reduced to a 3-CIG and became 1499 in late 2004, for initial use on the Lymington Branch line (see later in this volume). 25 November 2003.

Seen from the once very popular Alexander footbridge, just outside of Weymouth station, this is Class 423 4-VEP 3559, departing with an unknown working, possibly empty stock. Back in the days of steam, Weymouth Motive Power Depot (MPD) was situated behind the photographer and this bridge was ideal for observing the comings and goings of locos to/from Weymouth station. The bridge is still there today, but is unfortunately now one of those awful 'caged' examples. Although photography is just possible, it is very difficult to get clear shots. The unit succumbed to withdrawal in May 2004. 20 November 2003.

The Weymouth MPD mentioned in the previous image was situated to the right of this shot, but is now a housing estate. This is Class 411 4-CEP 1698 approaching Weymouth leading 1Z11, the 05.56 Ramsgate to Weymouth 'The Southern Belle' operated by South Eastern Trains/Southern Electric Group. Although this was not the final Southern Region third-rail network slam-door train to run, it was the final run on the South Western Division, and also for this leading unit, which was the very last 4-CEP to operate on the national network. The other two units in this formation were Class 423 4-VEP 3545 and Class 421 4-CIG 1866. As these two were Eastern section-allocated units, it is very doubtful they were ever seen this far south on the South Western Division prior to this charter. 17 September 2005.

Veteran 4-CEP 1698 is seen 'on the blocks' at Weymouth platform 3 after arrival with the charter outlined in the previous shot. 17 September 2005.

The headboard has now been attached to the other end of the train at Weymouth, where we see Class 421 4-CIG 1866 ready to take the train out later in the afternoon. This unit was withdrawn in November 2005. 17 September 2005.

This was also the last slam-door EMU ever to leave Weymouth and the occasion was marked by making sure all the doors on the 4-VEP were open when the train was in the station. If there is one thing 4-VEPs will be remembered for, it was the fact they had an awful lot of doors! 17 September 2005.

The final view of this historic charter was taken on the steep climb out of Weymouth with 1Z23, the 15.08 Weymouth to Ramsgate, now led by Class 421 4-CIG 1866 through this well-known location on the approach to Bincombe Tunnel. This was one of the favourite vantage points for photographers back in the days of steam when locos could be seen, often at walking pace, working hard hauling 12-coach trains, sometimes with another loco banking on the rear. The embankment here was far clearer than this, though. In more recent years, some clearance has taken place but it is generally still akin to a rainforest! Of course, these days the Weymouth relief road is also located to the left of picture, which has somewhat transformed the scenery hereabouts. 17 September 2005.

Much further up the South Western main line, we come to Winchester, where Class 412 4-CEP 2314 has just passed beneath the distinctive three bridges and is arriving with a Portsmouth to London Waterloo service. After the removal of one of the coaches, this unit was reconfigured as 3-CIG 1198 in mid-2004 for use on the Lymington branch. However, it only worked for around six months in this guise before being withdrawn in December 2004. This was not the end for the unit, however; it was initially hauled by 66701 from Eastleigh to the Dartmoor Railway but, after a couple more moves to heritage lines, it can currently be found on the Chinnor & Princes Risborough Railway. 9 February 2004.

This is Class 421 4-CIG 'Greyhound' 1319 leading a London Waterloo to Basingstoke stopping service into its destination. This unit was withdrawn from service just three weeks after this image was taken. 4 January 2005.

Another series of South Eastern images now as Class 423 4-VEP 3548 is seen at London Waterloo (East) on the rear of a service bound for Charing Cross. The Millennium Wheel, then still a fairly recent addition to the London skyline, can just be made out in the background. The unit was removed from service in August 2005. 13 November 2003.

A relatively smart-looking South Central two-tone green and white Class 421 4-CIG, 1856, is seen here departing from Clapham Junction on the rear of a London Victoria bound service. I think there were only ever about seven or eight 4-CIG units outshopped in this livery. It was withdrawn in April 2005. 11 February 2004.

The differing paintwork denotes some tell-tale juggling of coaches within Class 423 4-VEP 3842, seen leading a 12-coach formation on the approach to Horley soon after departing Gatwick Airport (just glimpsed in the distance) with a train for London Victoria. This unit was withdrawn in July 2005. 11 February 2004.

Left: Also approaching Horley from the Gatwick Airport direction, this is Class 423 4-VEP 3412 on the local line with a stopping train for London. This unit was withdrawn in August 2005. 11 February 2004.

Below: Class 421 4-CIG 1809 heads west through the centre line at Tonbridge with an unidentified service. Just a month later, it would be withdrawn in mid-December 2003. 13 November 2003.

Rather surprisingly, of all the Class 423 4-VEPs that were still in service at the time, this was the only one ever to receive the South Central two-tone green and white livery. 3514 is seen at Worthing with an unidentified service heading east. The painting of units in this new livery was abandoned due to the imminent entry into service of the Class 377s. The 4-VEP was withdrawn in November 2005. 3 December 2003.

At Barnham we see Class 421 4-CIG 1868 calling with another unidentified service heading east. This unit was withdrawn in May 2005. This station is the junction for the short line to Bognor Regis. 3 December 2003.

Coming off the line from Redhill is Class 421 4-CIG 1746, approaching Tonbridge station with an empty stock working. The wide expanse of Tonbridge engineers' yard (still very much in use today) can be found beyond the signal box above the unit. This unit succumbed to withdrawal in August 2004. 13 November 2003.

Moving back to the Southampton area, we arrive at Millbrook (Hants) to see Class 421 4-CIG 'Greyhound' 1395 leading another 4-CIG past the station with a London Waterloo to Weymouth fast service. This pair was being used as a stand in for a non-available Class 442 'Wessex Electric' unit, not an unusual occurrence at the time. Note also the Freightliner Class 08 shunter in the background. 1395 was withdrawn in May 2005. 5 March 2004.

Looking in the other direction from the same bridge as in the previous shot, we see a full 12-car Class 423 4-VEP combination, led by 3456, past the Freightliner terminal with a Poole to London Waterloo semi-fast service. 3456 was withdrawn during April 2005. 18 February 2005.

It is interesting to note the subtle differences between the two liveries here; Class 423 4-VEP 3415 still carries the base Network South East livery without the branding as it leads a sister unit in South West Trains livery past Millbrook (Hants) with a London Waterloo to Weymouth fast service, exemplifying another Class 442 substitution. This unit was withdrawn in February 2005. 26 November 2004.

A wider angle at Millbrook (Hants) as Class 421 4-CIG 1889 passes the Freightliner terminal with a train bound for London Waterloo. This unit was taken out of service in January 2005. 30 March 2004.

Coming around the curve on the approach to Southampton Central is Class 423 4-VEP 3467 with a Poole to London Waterloo semi-fast train. This unit was withdrawn in February 2005. 5 February 2004.

A never-to-be-repeated view at Southampton Central as we see Class 423 4-VEP 3519 to the left, forming a stopping service to Portsmouth, whilst to the right is a Class 442 'Wessex Electric' unit forming a service to London Waterloo. 3519 was withdrawn in May 2004 and the Class 442 succumbed not long after that. 26 October 2003.

Coming out of the down siding at Southampton is Class 412 4-CEP 2315, which is probably going to form the front part of a semi-fast service up from Poole. The fate of this unit was outlined earlier in the book. 2 September 2004.

A 12-coach semi-fast Poole to London Waterloo formation is led through St Denys station by Class 423 4-VEP 3812. Not long after this shot was taken, a start was made to refurbish the historic footbridge, which spans four lines. Unit withdrawn in March 2005. 27 January 2005.

Having just crossed from the main Weymouth and Southampton main line to London Waterloo, Class 423 4-VEP 3822 is approaching St Denys with a service for London Victoria. The footbridge visible directly above the third coach was removed not long after this shot was taken, but the road bridge behind is still there. This unit was withdrawn in August 2005, but was then purchased for preservation at the Churnet Valley Railway and used for a short while as non-powered loco-hauled coaching stock. However, due to persistent vandalism and thefts of essential parts, it was decided to scrap it, and this was carried out in 2010. 4 December 2003.

Still at St Denys, this is Class 421 4-CIG 1860 in the South Central two-tone green and white livery with another service for London Victoria. The state of the track here at this time left something to be desired! It has long since been renewed, thankfully, even though the unit was withdrawn in July 2005. 13 May 2004.

An unusual one here as we see Class 421 4-CIG 1853 soon after leaving Southampton Central and approaching Mount Pleasant Road crossing on its way to London Victoria. The unit is in plain white, which only a few received prior to a new livery being decided upon whilst franchises changed over. It went on to receive the scheme sported by the unit in the previous image, but in March 2005 was withdrawn. 11 October 2004.

Approaching Mount Pleasant Road crossing from the opposite direction is Class 423 4-VEP 3407, leading a London Waterloo to Weymouth fast service. This would have been another Class 442 'Wessex Electric' substitute. It was withdrawn in April 2005. 7 October 2004.

Here is Class 421 4-CIG 'Greyhound' 1398 leading a semi-fast London Waterloo to Poole service away from Eastleigh. The fresh appearance of the ballast and trackwork is a sign that extensive works had recently taken place here to renew this junction. The unit was withdrawn in May 2005, but one of its coaches has been preserved and was initially moved to West Bay (Dorset); more about this later in the book. 20 April 2005.

Southern Slammers: The Final Years

The telephoto lens emphasises the bending of this 12-coach formation led by Class 423 4-VEP 3401 as it departs from platform 3 at Eastleigh with a London Waterloo to Portsmouth train. The unit was withdrawn in April 2005. 24 January 2005.

Another 12-coach train, this time formed of Class 421 4-CIG units, is led out of Eastleigh by 1304 with a London Waterloo to Poole semi-fast service. Unfortunately, the nice tidy area between the depot line in the foreground and the main running lines has, in recent years, become something of a forest of *Buddleja* bushes that do get cut down occasionally, but then just grow back stronger and quicker every time! The unit was withdrawn in April 2005, in fact just three days after this shot. 20 April 2005.

Main Lines – South and East

Further east on the South Western Main Line, Class 411 4-CEP 1550 is on the approach to Basingstoke with a Portsmouth to London Waterloo service. This unit was withdrawn from service nine days after this image was taken. 9 January 2004.

Here we see Class 423 4-VEP 3508 leading an empty stock train through Basingstoke. Since the date of this shot, the platform through which it is passing has been extended somewhat. One of the new order is seen in the adjacent platform in the form of 'Desiro' 450055. 3508 was withdrawn in November 2004.

To round off the first section of this volume. we have a brief section in my home county of Dorset. This is Class 423 4-VEP 3810, calling at Pokesdown with a stopping service from Wareham to Brockenhurst. This view was taken from the very high footbridge located here. Apparent from this image is the large space between the up and down lines, due to there being two through lines prior to remodelling in the late 1960s when the third-rail electrification was introduced. In recent years, the station has been renamed 'Pokesdown for Boscombe'. The unit was withdrawn in March 2005. 15 September 2004.

Bournemouth T&RSMD is a large depot and carriage sidings complex that was developed upon the closure of Bournemouth West terminus station in the late 1960s to maintain the new electric stock that was gradually entering service at that time. A new shed was built on the track bed of the former main line, but an older carriage shed that had existed prior to this was retained for stabling and cleaning purposes. In this telephoto view from the former Branksome signal box, we see withdrawn Class 411 4-CEP 1527 in a very woebegone state, dumped in a siding that was once the location of Branksome MPD in the days of steam. The remains of an unidentified unit are behind it. The two original main lines (to the right of shot) were retained here and now form the ingoing and outgoing lines to the depot. 1527 was withdrawn as long ago as April 1999, but was stored here at Bournemouth, presumably for spare parts. It was finally disposed of in June 2004. 7 December 2003.

48

Moving west of Poole, Class 423 4-VEP 3402 is crossing the causeway at Holes Bay, between Poole and Hamworthy, with a Brockenhurst to Wareham stopping service. This is a hot spot for bird life in the area and can sometimes throw up some real rarities. The unit was withdrawn in April 2005. 18 October 2004.

Another view at Holes Bay, this time from the road bridge over the line. Class 423 4-VEP 3411 approaches with a Wareham to Brockenhurst stopping service on a misty day. Part of the obvious attractiveness of this area can be appreciated in this view. The unit was withdrawn in March 2005. 7 February 2005.

Southern Slammers: The Final Years

The same unit as in the previous view, this time seen departing away from the camera at Hamworthy station with a Brockenhurst to Wareham stopping train. At the time, the semaphore signal to the left was the only one on the main line between London Waterloo and Weymouth, but all was not what it seemed. It was retained only as a reminder for trains going down the branch line to Hamworthy Goods that was accessed via a loop line out of sight to the left, that they must stop before proceeding. It was not connected to the signalling system in any way at this time and has since been removed. 28 January 2005.

Looking in the opposite direction at Hamworthy station, we see Class 423 4-VEP 3456 departing with a Wareham to Poole stopping train. It is hard to believe that just to the left of the train was the junction of the original main line that used to go via Wimborne/Ringwood and join the Bournemouth main line at Lymington Junction. The unit was withdrawn from service in April 2005. 28 January 2005.

A few minutes before the heavens opened, Class 421 4-CIG 'Greyhound' 1393 is about to depart Hamworthy with another Wareham to Brockenhurst stopping train. The signal box in view was, by this time, only used when there was a train due to go down the branch to Hamworthy Goods, about three miles distant. However, upon the Dorset Coast resignalling project, the box was closed in May 2014 and soon after demolished, although the branch line has stayed intact. Details for the unit were set out earlier in this volume. 4 March 2005.

Apart from celebrity unit 4-VEP 3417, there was nothing else in the way of special liveries during the last few months of slam-door EMU workings. This, however, is Class 412 4-CEP 2313, complete with white buffers, arriving at Wareham after exiting the sidings just beyond the flyover in the background. I suspect this was done by someone who remembered the last days of steam when some locos were also adorned with white buffers, especially on the Southern Region. This unit was withdrawn in October 2004, a month after this shot. 9 September 2004.

Another view of 4-CEP 2313 at Wareham, now awaiting departure with a stopping train for Brockenhurst. 9 September 2004.

Taken from the signal box at Dorchester South, this is Class 412 4-CEP 2317, departing east with a Weymouth to London Waterloo service. I suspect this unit was either taken out of service at Bournemouth in favour of a Class 442 'Wessex Electric' or was joined by another unit for the continuation of the journey to London. In any case, it was withdrawn in September 2004. 18 May 2004.

To the left is the signal box from which the previous shot was taken as Class 421 4-CIG 'Greyhound' departs Dorchester South with a Weymouth to Bournemouth stopping service. This unit was withdrawn in April 2005. 24 March 2004.

Chapter 2
Lymington Branch (The Heritage Line)

After the withdrawal of slam-door EMUs from all of the Southern Region operating areas at the end of 2005, the only place on the network to see these veterans at work was on the almost six-mile branch line from Brockenhurst to Lymington in Hampshire. Two former 4-CIG units were reduced to 3-CIG Nos 1497+1498 by the removal of one coach and the fitment of central door locking and were used until May 2010. They also received heritage liveries and official names in a ceremony at Brockenhurst station when 1497 was christened *Freshwater* and 1498 *Farringford*. This section is dedicated to what was originally advertised as 'The Heritage Line' and mainly shows these two units in a variety of locations on this line. The line was also in the news just over 40 years previously, as it was the last steam-worked branch line in the country.

Prior to May 2005, standard four-coach units worked the line, including 4-CIGs/4-CEPs/4-VEPs. This is Class 421 4-CIG 'Greyhound' 1398 departing Brockenhurst with a Lymington-bound train. These standard four-coach units were, however, a bit too long for Lymington Town and Pier stations, hence the creation of dedicated three-coach units for the line by removing a coach from existing units. Note the small headboard that was made by an enthusiastic employee and was often used by local crews. 9 July 2004.

I have included this shot away from the branch as it is the only reasonable image I have of this particular unit. Class 411 3-CEP 1199 is seen passing Southampton Central with an unknown working, but possibly a turning move. This was the first unit to be adapted for the branch by the removal of a coach, being converted from 4-CEP 2326 in early 2003 and lasting in service for just over a year. 6 September 2003.

The next example to be adapted to work the branch line was Class 411 3-CEP 1198, which was converted from 4-CEP 2314 in mid-2004. It is seen here departing Brockenhurst for Lymington, whilst on the main line in the distance is an echo of the past in the form of Bulleid 'West Country' Pacific 34027 *Taw Valley* (running at this time as long-lost sister 34045 *Ottery St Mary*) with a 'Sunny South Special' charter bound for Weymouth. 1198 was withdrawn in December 2004, but was later preserved on the Chinnor & Princes Risborough Railway. 1 September 2004.

Another shot of 1198 in the down loop at Brockenhurst, which is the usual platform used by the Lymington trains. They do sometimes use the up loop, but much more rarely. 18 August 2004.

With the painting of Class 423 4-VEP 3417 *Gordon Pettitt* in all-over BR blue livery during 2004, it was inevitable that it would appear on the branch at some point. Here we see the unit approaching Brockenhurst with a service from Lymington. 14 July 2004.

Displaying the correct route code of 97 for the branch, this is a close-up study of 4-VEP 3417 *Gordon Pettitt*, standing at Brockenhurst awaiting departure to Lymington. In early 2024, moves were advancing to get this unit main-line registered again, so, fingers crossed, it will soon be seen out and about on the third-rail network once again in the not-too-distant future. 14 July 2004.

Another view of 4-VEP 3417 *Gordon Pettitt* at Brockenhurst. The footbridge to the right of the picture is actually nothing to do with the station; although it spans all lines and platforms, there is no access from it to any of them. It has been very handy for photographers over the years, though! 14 July 2004.

The final unit to be converted before the two dedicated units came into service was Class 421 3-CIG 1499, originally Class 421 4-CIG 1394. This unit only operated on the line for around five or six months, but is captured here at the divergence of the branch line away from the main Bournemouth line at what was Lymington Junction. Originally, there was a physical connection to the main line at this point, with a signal box in the vee to the right of the train in this view, but the location was remodelled during 1978 when the signalling was updated and the box removed. 8 January 2005.

Now a series of images taken to accompany the commencement of the five-year-long 'heritage line' status that the line enjoyed from 2005 to 2010. Mentioned earlier was the up loop at Brockenhurst station. This is 3-CIG 1499 in this loop after arriving from Lymington. As this was the day of the launch of the two newly refurbished units, 1499 had to use this loop (platform 1) to free up space for the naming of 1497+1498 and their subsequent entry into service, which occurred at platform 4. 12 May 2005.

Arriving at Brockenhurst for their naming ceremony and entry into traffic from Bournemouth Depot are immaculate 3-CIG pair 1497+1498, both with covered nameplates. The pair had to run into the main up platform to be able to gain access to the down loop via a crossover at the western end of the station. 12 May 2005.

It's goodbye to 3-CIG 1499, which is seen waiting to leave Brockenhurst for Bournemouth Depot and withdrawal from service, whilst behind we see 1497 ready to enter service with a departure for Lymington. 12 May 2005.

1498 *Farringford*, with 1497 *Freshwater* behind, are seen during the twin naming ceremonies at Brockenhurst, whilst some of the train crew for that day are busy having a chat. 12 May 2005.

A close-up of 1498 *Farringford* at Brockenhurst, including that headboard again. 12 May 2005.

Once the naming ceremonies and speeches were completed, both units worked the first couple of trains from Brockenhurst to Lymington together. This is thought to be the only time they actually worked together as a pair on the line. The usual working practice was one unit on maintenance and the other working the branch. However, sometimes things didn't go according to plan and a Class 450 'Desiro' was occasionally drafted in. In this case, both units are crossing the heathland expanse of Setley Plain, about five minutes or so from Brockenhurst, as they make for Lymington. 12 May 2005.

The six-mile branch line itself has only one intermediate station at Lymington Town these days, but originally there were two other halts at Shirley Holms (closed as long ago as 1888) and at Ampress Works Halt. Today, there is no sign of Shirley Holms Halt, but the one at Ampress Works still exists, or at least it did in 2005 when I took this shot. I have not been there since, so I am not sure if it is still extant. It was also quite tricky to photograph this former halt, as there is no longer any official access to it except by scrambling through a woodland and straining to look over a boundary fence. The halt was only ever a single platform and was provided essentially for workers at a large nearby engineering factory, now long since closed. This tiny and little-known station was never even advertised in any rail timetables, although the public could actually use it, if they wished. In later years, it was just known as 'Ampress' and was closed completely in 1989. The train seen in the previous shot, now led by 1497 *Freshwater*, is seen passing the closed halt on its way from Lymington to Brockenhurst. 12 May 2005.

Although not obvious from this angle, 1498 *Farringford* + 1497 *Freshwater* are seen deep in the heavily wooded area south of Shirley Holms with a Brockenhurst to Lymington service. Obtaining this shot also required a hike through some very awkward terrain! 12 May 2005.

The last shot taken on the launch day sees 1497 *Freshwater* now running solo as it passes near Shirley Holms with a service for Lymington. Note the old concrete permanent way hut to the right; made in their thousands at the long-gone Exmouth Junction concrete works near Exeter, these could once be found all over the Southern Region. 12 May 2005.

1498 *Farringford* is about to depart Brockenhurst with the 11.50 service to Lymington. 26 August 2005.

Here we see 1497 *Freshwater* arriving at Lymington Town station with a service for Lymington Pier. The station here once had the luxury of an overall roof, but it was removed many years ago. There also used to be a goods yard here and even a small steam depot. Today, there is just the single track and a single platform. 28 November 2007.

Southern Slammers: The Final Years

The end of the line, quite literally, is at Lymington Pier, where we see 1497 *Freshwater* just terminated with a service from Brockenhurst. The railway makes a very convenient connection here for ferries to the Isle of Wight, and one of these can be seen in the background. Back in the days of steam, run-round facilities for locos were provided here, and some well-known images from those days show that the buffer stops were almost overhanging the seashore, so any misjudged movements or lateness on the brakes here could easily have seen the steam loco drop into the sea! Nowadays, as can be appreciated here, the ferry comes right up close to the end of the line with a slipway provided for passengers to board; the actual track is now some distance short of the sea. 28 November 2007.

A view of 1497 *Freshwater* from the opposite end of Lymington Pier. This station again used to be adorned with proper canopies and station buildings, but these were all swept away in the late 1960s and now all that is here is a small flimsy shelter to protect you from the elements. It will also be noted that halfway up the closest lamp post, there is a replica station identification sign of the type originally to be seen all over the railway system. These were added at all three stations on this line as a part of the 'heritage' theme. 28 November 2007.

Lymington Branch (The Heritage Line)

Undoubtedly the most interesting location for photographing this line is in the area between Lymington Town and Lymington Pier stations, where the line crosses a short bridge over the Lymington River. There is also a very busy marina here with many boats in the area, especially in the summer months. 1497 *Freshwater* has just crossed the bridge (out of sight to the left of shot) and is seen approaching Lymington Pier station with a service from Brockenhurst. 28 November 2007.

In fine early autumn light, this is 1497 *Freshwater* again, this time crossing the bridge with a Brockenhurst to Lymington train. This is a very pleasant area on a fine day for just sitting and enjoying the sunshine or messing about in boats. 26 September 2008.

This time we see 1498 *Farringford* crossing the bridge with a Lymington Pier to Brockenhurst service. Although it is not readily apparent in this shot, the bridge is actually on quite a curve and, with rather an intensive service for a single line with trains every half an hour each way, the rails suffer a good degree of wear. 31 May 2005.

With the inevitable seagulls dotted all around, 1498 *Farringford* has just departed Lymington Pier and is approaching the bridge with a service for Brockenhurst, just over a month before the unit's withdrawal from the line. 1 April 2010.

With the 216ft (626m) high Sway Tower on the skyline and an archetypal New Forest pony in the foreground, 1498 *Farringford* is crossing the open heath of Setley Plain and approaching Lymington Junction with a Lymington to Brockenhurst service. 9 July 2009.

In July 2008 the 150th anniversary of the opening of the line was celebrated and South West Trains (SWT) marked the occasion by providing a Class 73 loco to work with the 3-CIG units for a weekend. Since the end of steam operations on the line, any sort of loco has always been rare on the branch, and visits in recent years have been restricted to the occasional overnight Network Rail test trains. In this image we see 1498 *Farringford* being propelled away from Brockenhurst by Class 73/1 No 73109 *Battle of Britain – 50th Anniversary* with a Lymington-bound train on the exact date of the opening of the branch some 150 years previously. 12 July 2008.

The same pairing as in the previous image is seen soon after, veering away from the main line at Lymington Junction with another Brockenhurst to Lymington service. In the background is the main London Waterloo to Bournemouth and Weymouth line, passing over what is locally known as 'skew bridge'. 12 July 2008.

Back to solo units now and we are at the former Lymington Junction again to see 1498 *Farringford* heading along the last mile or so to Brockenhurst station with a service from Lymington. Although the physical connection here was removed in 1978, this location is still referred to as Lymington Junction in railway circles.
2 August 2006.

Left: Looking in the opposite direction to the previous shot, we see 1497 *Freshwater* coming along the independent line from Brockenhurst with a service for Lymington on a fine early spring afternoon. The up and down main lines from London Waterloo to Weymouth are in the foreground.
2 March 2010.

Below: On the same day, and with the sun now starting to set, 1497 *Freshwater* is seen at Lymington Junction again, on its return from Lymington with a service for Brockenhurst.
2 March 2010.

This shot really backs up the need for door locks on slam-door trains. As 1497 *Freshwater* comes around the curve towards Shirley Holms with a Brockenhurst to Lymington service, the first door on the unit can clearly be seen as not being closed properly. Although it would still have been locked on a secondary catch, it should not have been overlooked back at Brockenhurst, but it was quite an easy thing to miss. Apart from a few exemptions, the requirement for door locks to be fitted to slam-door stock on the main line came into force at the end of 2005, and both 1497 and 1498 were so fitted, enabling them to operate beyond this deadline. 16 April 2010.

Although it is called the New Forest, much of this National Park is made up of heathland. This is very apparent here as 1497 *Freshwater* is seen framed by the only tree for some distance on the approaches to Lymington Junction, this time returning from Lymington to Brockenhurst across the large expanse of Setley Plain. 16 April 2010.

There is no doubt of the location here as 1497 *Freshwater* arrives at its destination with a train from Brockenhurst. Out of sight to the right of shot is a large car park from where vehicles queue to board the ferries. 28 November 2007.

With the driver changing ends, 1498 *Farringford* has just arrived at the usual platform 4 at Brockenhurst with a service from Lymington. There was only about ten minutes' turnaround time at each end of the line, so any late running was not likely to be made up very easily; in fact, if any service ran too late, the next one was often cancelled to try and get things back to time. 31 May 2005.

The only intermediate station on the line nowadays is Lymington Town, which, as the title says, is the station for the town itself, just a short walk away. 1498 *Farringford* is calling with a service for Lymington Pier. Note again there is another door on the catch; however, this was remedied quite soon, as it was the point where I boarded for the short trip to the pier station! The unit is also carrying a blank headcode, as was sometimes the case, perhaps when the driver was not that familiar with local arrangements. 1 April 2010.

Witnessed by a small boat serving as a planter for daffodils, 1498 *Farringford* has now arrived at Lymington Pier and is ready for the trip back to Brockenhurst. Foot passengers for the ferry to Yarmouth, Isle of Wight, will have a short walk from the wooden platform here to just behind the camera where the ferry will be moored. 1 April 2010.

After four years working the branch, 1498 *Farringford*, again showing a blank headcode, is now looking a bit work-worn as it approaches Shirley Holms with a Brockenhurst to Lymington train. 9 July 2009.

An arty look at 1498 *Farringford* through an old rusting buffer stop as it approaches Brockenhurst with a service from Lymington. The collection of items in the foreground are spare third-rail insulators, or 'pots' as they are commonly known. 9 July 2009.

From the original footbridge at Brockenhurst station (it was replaced in the mid-2010s), we see 1497 *Freshwater* arriving from Lymington. The old parcels van to the left was being used at the time by a bicycle hire company and has since been removed, while the cycle hire company is now located further down the track to the left of the van in this view. This specially constructed loading dock was originally used by motor-rail trains for a period from the mid-1970s to the early 1980s. They used to run between here and Kensington Olympia and then eventually on to Stirling in Scotland. Photos of these trains are very rare, unfortunately. 16 March 2010.

When the two 3-CIGs were introduced on the line, the waiting room at Brockenhurst station on platforms 3 and 4 was enhanced with the addition of some older views of the station and nearby locations. I have not been here for some years, so am not sure if it is still so adorned. 1497 *Freshwater* is glimpsed through the window, awaiting departure for Lymington. 20 December 2006.

To round off this section on the Lymington branch, we see the beginning and (almost) the end of the 'heritage' years. This is 1497 *Freshwater*, just after its naming ceremony on the launch day at Brockenhurst platform 4. 12 May 2005.

At the same spot almost five years later, 1497 *Freshwater* again has just a month left to go in service; the modified headboard says it all. Both 3-CIGs were taken out of service on 22 May 2010 when they were replaced initially by SWT Class 158 two-car diesel units during weekdays and Class 450 'Desiro' units at weekends. More recently, the service has been worked solidly with Class 450s. Thankfully the two 3-CIGs went on to be preserved. 1497 went to the Mid Norfolk Railway, but then moved on to the Spa Valley Railway, where it can be seen in service today, though obviously used as normal coaching stock. 1498 was first moved to the Epping Ongar Railway but, in a bizarre move during 2016, it was bought by a businessman in County Sligo, Ireland, for his Quirky Nights Glamping Village! It is not in railway service but used as unusual sleeping accommodation for guests. At least it survived the scrapman! 21 April 2010.

Chapter 3

Loco Hauled/Propelled

Main Line and Heritage

This section focuses on various EMUs that have been hauled (or propelled) by locos on the main line and also on the Swanage Railway during the popular diesel galas, and at other times. Class 491 4TC (later Class 438) units were not actually self-powered, but they were designed to work in conjunction with EMU stock, primarily on the Bournemouth line between Bournemouth and Weymouth, although they were also regular visitors to Salisbury/Portsmouth and Reading. Many of the separate coaches within these units were regularly juggled around whilst in service, so to go into any great detail would fill a book the size of the UK! I have also not given withdrawal dates this time, as many individual coaches of these units saw further use, scrapping or preservation and things all became rather complicated.

To commence the last section of this volume, we see Class 491 4-TC 408 leading another 4-TC and powered from the rear by a Class 432 4-REP with a London Waterloo to Bournemouth semi-fast service about to call at Southampton Central. 4-REP units were the most powerful EMUs on BR at the time, producing almost the same power as the famous (and perhaps more glamorous!) 3,300hp 'Deltic' diesel locos used on the East Coast Main Line between London and Scotland. Circa 1985.

This was the classic Class 33/1 and 4-TC (or 2 x 4-TC) combination that ruled the Bournemouth to Weymouth route between 1967 and 1988. In this shot, 33113 and Class 491 4-TCs 422+409 head south through Holton Heath with a London Waterloo to Weymouth service. Back then, this station was rarely used, with only a couple of trains per day stopping here. In recent years, a large industrial estate has developed in the vicinity and the train service is now more or less hourly each way to cater for this. 14 July 1985.

With the Swanage branch bearing off to the left, 33119 and Class 491 4-TC 416 pass Worgret Junction, just south of Wareham, with a London Waterloo to Weymouth service. At this time, the branch only ran as far as Furzebrook Sidings, from where oil trains regularly travelled to/from South Wales. 2 June 1985.

Towards the end of their service, the Class 491 units were renumbered and reclassified as Class 438s. This view depicts 4-TC 8029 with another unidentified unit behind, and the inevitable Class 33/1 behind that again, heading away from Poole and climbing the 1-in-50 incline towards Parkstone with a Weymouth to London Waterloo service. These two units would have coupled up to a Class 432 4-REP at Bournemouth, with the Class 33/1 then removed from the rear and the train continuing on to its destination as a 12-coach formation. The land here in the foreground was reclaimed in the early 1970s, right up to the track side that actually marked the original coastline, but it was on a shallow reinforced concrete embankment at this point, which is now buried beneath the infilling. Circa 1987.

During late 1987/early 1988, I had some involvement with the electrification work on the Bournemouth to Weymouth line and visited some pretty awkward places that were virtually impossible to get to as a member of the public, even if you were allowed. One such spot is seen here in the deep cutting at the northern end of Bincombe Tunnel, which lies between Dorchester and Upwey. 4-TCs 8022+8030, propelled by 33111 (now preserved on the nearby Swanage Railway), are seen breasting the long climb from Weymouth with a service for London Waterloo. You can actually gauge how severe this climb is in this image, and also the exertions of the Class 33 on the rear. To the right of shot can be seen the recess that used to house the very isolated Bincombe signal box. This was primarily used back in steam days, when there used to be a short refuge siding and crossover between the tracks here for the regular banking locos that assisted heavy trains up this incline, before they returned light engine back to Weymouth. Although this box was closed in March 1970, it remained intact for some years after, until demolition occurred in the 1980s. To access this box, the signaller was first expected to cross an open field and then take this precarious path to reach his place of work. Bad enough in the daylight, but just imagine having to do that in the dark and during inclement weather; it doesn't bear thinking about! To underscore the inaccessibility of this location, the rare and high-quality bricks that were used to build the signal box many years ago had to be left as there was no easy way to recover them, hence they are just dumped in a big heap since the day of demolition! The tunnel itself is reputedly haunted, but in all the times I have carried out track patrols through it, I never encountered any spooky goings-on! In the winter months, however, large icicles formed inside the tunnel roof, and on more than one occasion drivers' cab windows were broken by them. 23 November 1987.

About a mile north of the previous shot, we see 4-TC 8012 being propelled by 33114 past the long-closed Monkton & Came Halt on the way to Dorchester with a Weymouth to London Waterloo service. This small halt was located just out of sight to the left of shot. It was opened way back in 1905 by the GWR (the stretch of line from Dorchester Junction to Weymouth having been constructed by the GWR) and was mainly intended for golfers using the course located a few miles from here, but was not used much and closed in 1957. The two original platforms still just about exist. 23 November 1987.

We saw this classic location in the first section of this book, but an awful lot more overgrown. Class 438s 8006+80XX are being slowly propelled up the steep incline towards Bincombe Tunnel with a Weymouth to London Waterloo service. Two 4-TC units consisting of eight coaches were pretty heavy work for a Class 33 with only 1,550hp, and really taxed them up this long steep gradient. To the left of shot, just out of view, was the delightfully named Wishing Well Halt, also opened by the GWR back in 1905 but closed in 1957, although the platforms lasted a lot longer. 23 November 1987.

A Dorset station that is still open but not often photographed is Moreton, between Wool and Dorchester South. 4-TC 8021, being propelled by 33106, arrives with a Weymouth to London Waterloo service. This was the final weekday of push-pull operation on this route before the Class 442 'Wessex Electrics' took over. 13 May 1988.

Around two miles north of Moreton, this is another shot on the final weekday of push-pull operations. 4-TCs 8026+8025 are being propelled by 33101 near Winfrith. There is a nuclear establishment here that used to generate semi-regular trains to remove the waste materials up until the early 1990s, but this traffic ceased for many years until the early 2020s when it was revived, using Class 68 locos operated by Direct Rail Services (DRS). I believe this too has recently ended. The heathland and woodland is lovely in this part of the countryside, with very few dwellings. 13 May 1988.

This shot was taken midway between the previous shot and Moreton station, an area locally known as Redbridge. Here we see 4-TCs 8004+8028 being propelled by 33114 *Sultan* soon after leaving Moreton with a Weymouth to London Waterloo service. The leading unit was the only 4-TC to receive the Network South East livery then being applied en masse. It is also unusual in that one of the driving coaches (76275) later went on to be included in 4-VEP 3582. The coach has now been preserved for eventual use on the Swanage Railway in the formation of a complete 4-TC. The other unit, 8028, is also preserved and is now based at the London Underground depot at West Ruislip. 13 May 1988.

It was not only Class 33/1s that could operate in push-pull mode with 4-TCs. Class 73/1 and 73/2 could also be seen around the Southern network, operating in the same way. This shot, taken from the former signal box at Branksome, has three 4-TCs in view but the only one identifiable is 8106, behind 73110. This was one of a few renumbered at this time to reflect the addition of a modified coach within the consist. 'Inter-City'-liveried 73110 is waiting to haul them down the short double-tracked line to Bournemouth Depot, just out of sight to the left. Meanwhile, 'large logo'-liveried 73114 is about to head north the three miles or so to Bournemouth, to form the front of a train from Weymouth. 17 February 1988.

Another location that is certainly an off-limits area for the public is seen here as 73130 hauls an eight-coach formation across the Surrey Road viaduct towards Bournemouth, just after departing from Branksome. At this time, almost daily shuffling and reforming of units was occurring, and today the first unit has the addition of a buffet car, probably removed from one of the Class 432 4-REP units that were gradually removed from service to yield parts for the new Class 442 'Wessex Electrics' entering service during 1988. Behind my position here was the junction for the line that used to cross the other Surrey Road viaduct (still in situ in 2024 to the left of shot) and go direct to what used to be Bournemouth West terminus station. This short spur line was closed in the late 1960s and over the years there has been talk of reopening it so as to make it easier to access Bournemouth Depot rather than having to reverse at Branksome. As usual, though, nothing has come of this. 18 March 1987.

In September 1991, 4-TC 410 was returned to a condition as close as possible (including original number) to when it was first released to traffic back in the mid-1960s and painted in all-over BR blue livery. Its restoration was to accompany intended use on special services and charter trains, but this did not really get off the ground and the unit was eventually split up, with some coaches sold on for further use and others scrapped. Here we see 410 being propelled by 73109 *Battle of Britain – 50th Anniversary* (out of sight) passing just south of Wool with a special train heading for Weymouth Quay for clearance testing in advance of some upcoming charters. 25 March 1993.

The train in the previous shot spent most of the day at Weymouth Quay before returning to Bournemouth Depot. 73109 *Battle of Britain – 50th Anniversary* now leads 4-TC 410 soon after leaving Dorchester South towards home. Both of these shots were taken from non-public areas. 25 March 1993.

Moving on a few years to the mid-2000s, slam-door EMUs were again to be seen being hauled or propelled around the Southern Region network. The Lymington branch 3-CIGs were occasionally turned on the Eastleigh–Fareham–Southampton triangle so as to even up flange wear on the wheels that occurred when working continuously on the same stretch of line. This is 3-CIG 1497 *Freshwater*, propelled by an immaculate SWT-liveried 73201 past Millbrook FLT with just such a move. 23 August 2005.

A little later in the day, the same duo are captured on their way back through Southampton Central, heading for Bournemouth Depot. I think the Class 73 went along just as a bit of insurance in case the unit failed. 23 August 2005.

In this view, we see Class 423 4-VEP 3417 *Gordon Pettitt and* 3-CIG 1497 *Freshwater*, hauled by an unidentified Class 73, passing through Christchurch with a maintenance move headed for Wimbledon Depot. Note the remains of a piece of long-lost railway history just in view to the left; the concrete frame of an old wagon-loading gauge was last used when this station had a goods yard, many years ago. 26 August 2005.

During the mid-to-late 2000s, the Lymington line units and in particular, Class 423 4-VEP 3417 *Gordon Pettitt*, were often used for driver training runs hauled/propelled by Class 73s. This is the latter approaching Poole, propelled by 73201. The curvature at this location is self-evident in the image. Up until the early 1970s, there were also two road crossings here in close proximity; one was just in front of the unit and the other, which is still used, but only by pedestrians nowadays, can just be seen under the Class 73. They apparently caused havoc with road users, even in those days! 22 March 2005.

In 2010, the ownership of Class 423 4-VEP 3417 *Gordon Pettitt* was transferred to the Bluebell Railway in Sussex. After some remedial maintenance at Bournemouth Depot, this is 73141 *Charlotte* + 73208 *Kirsten* + Vep 3417 *Gordon Pettit* + 73206 *Lisa* approaching Brockenhurst with 5Z73, the 11.28 Bournemouth T&RSMD to East Grinstead. 8 September 2011.

When the 4-TC units were withdrawn, many of the coaches were secured by preservationists and other operators. One such to gain a few was London Underground Ltd (LUL), based at West Ruislip. A complete 4-TC is sometimes used behind battery loco *Sarah Siddons* around the London area, but has also been lent to other operators for rail tours. Although it doesn't carry a running number, I believe it is allocated 8028, but not all vehicles in the set come from that unit originally. A good way of getting the unit to the 2014 Swanage diesel gala was to arrange a charter from the London area. In the rather drab teak livery, the unit is passing over the Mount Pleasant level crossing near Southampton with 1Z33, the 10.24 Ealing Broadway to Swanage 'The Purbeck Explorer 1' hauled by West Coast Railway-operated 33029 *Glen Loy*. This charter was originally to have been hauled by a Class 20, but some sort of dispute at the time precluded that from happening. 7 May 2014.

A few years later and the London Underground 4-TC has been repainted in a much more cheerful London Transport deep red livery. It is seen at the unlikely location of Oxford on the rear of 1Z73, the 07.14 London Paddington to Long Marston private GBRF charter tailed by 73962 *Dick Mabbutt* and led by 73963 *Janice* at this point. 20 June 2018.

Withdrawal from main-line services also caused many units to be stored at various locations around the south and east while they awaited a date with either the scrapman or preservationists. This is Class 423 4-VOP 3918 (with 3905) bringing up the rear of 5M23, the 09.04 Tonbridge West Yard to Barrow Hill, approaching Putney on their way north via the Midland Main Line. I think these were the last units stored in the south-east. Some parts of this particular unit were intended to be used in the project to restore a 5-BEL (Brighton Pullman) unit. 26 March 2013.

We now move to the Swanage Railway, where a number of slammers have been hauled by a selection of locos during the popular annual diesel galas over the years. To start, we have an unlikely selection heading towards the main line at the River Frome bridges, which is the limit for Swanage trains that are not booked to go forward to the main line at Worgret Junction. 73213+73212+56101+73119 *Borough of Eastleigh* +3417 *Gordon Pettitt* are working 5Z73, the 17.50 Motala Ground Frame to Eastleigh RC with returning gala attractions. Note that the two leading Class 73s are in the short-lived First livery, often known as 'Barbie'! 11 May 2010.

This time we see a charter that has come onto the Swanage Railway from the main line. 73201 *Broadlands* top-and-tailed with 73107 *Tracy* and sandwiching the immaculate London Underground Ltd 4-TC are crossing Corfe Common with 1Z73, the 09.44 London Waterloo to Swanage 'The Swanage Sunday Special No.1' organised by UK Railtours. 28 July 2019.

In recent years, Swanage has run its own services as far as Wareham on the national network, using a variety of stock and locos. In 2017, it was the turn of WCRC's 33025 and Swanage's own 33012 (D6515) *Lt Jenny Lewis RN* to do the honours, utilising the LUL 4TC. 33025 is seen here at Catseye Bridge on the less used extension, leading 2Z29, the 13.19 Wareham to Swanage train. 13 August 2017.

Later in the day, 33025, now on the rear of 2Z32, the 16.26 Swanage to Wareham service, was captured at Holme Lane, just south of Worgret Junction. More recently, this service has operated with the Swanage Railway's own main line-certified heritage DMU; although it has been quite well used, it was not quite such a draw as two locos and the 4-TC! 13 August 2017.

With a fine show of wild flowers in the foreground, 33103 *Swordfish* is hauling ex-Lymington 3-CIG 1498 *Farringford*, forming a Swanage to Norden service, on the approach to Corfe Castle station. This shot was not taken during a diesel gala, but both the loco and the unit were actually based here for a short while and worked some of the line's regular services. 8 June 2011.

Crossing over the attractive little viaduct at Corfe Castle with a Norden to Swanage service is the pioneer Class 37 loco, 37119 (D6700), hauling the LuL 4-TC during the time it carried the teak wood-effect livery. The Class 37 is currently owned by the NRM, but occasionally gets to stretch its legs on heritage lines. 9 May 2014.

Viewed from high on the Purbeck Hills, this is a sight that would have been almost impossible in the 1970s or 1980s; both of these items of BR rolling stock were worlds apart when in regular use. Class 55 Deltic 55002 *King's Own Yorkshire Light Infantry* hauls the LUL 4-TC past Woody Hyde camp site, soon after departing Harman's Cross with a Swanage to Norden service. The Class 55 is also owned by the NRM. 11 May 2014.

As strange as it may seem, this combination of 50035 *Ark Royal* and 4-VEP 3417 *Gordon Pettitt* could well have happened at some point in the 1980s or '90s. Class 50s certainly hauled 4-TC units from London Waterloo to Salisbury and sometimes even beyond to Exeter. Class 50/4-VEP would have been much rarer, but were not totally unknown. Also, 50s never ran in service in Loadhaul colours, and there was never a '50135' in those days! Many people frowned on this livery on a Class 50 but personally, I think it looked OK. The duo is seen just after departure from Harman's Cross with a shuttle service to Corfe Castle. 7 May 2010.

Southern Slammers: The Final Years

Above: With that unmistakeable and famous landmark prominent in the distance, 37264, top-and-tailing 73119 *Borough of Eastleigh*, have charge of 4-VEP 3417 *Gordon Pettitt* and are seen on the approach to Harman's Cross station with a terminating shuttle service from Corfe Castle. 9 May 2010.

Left: Another unusual combination, 33111 (then locally named *Hot Dog!*) + 31271 *Stratford 1840-2001* + 4-VEP 3417 *Gordon Pettitt* are crossing Corfe Viaduct with a Swanage to Norden service. 9 May 2010.

More bizarre combinations! This is another that was unlikely to have happened 'back in the day'. Captured here is Class 52 'Western' D1062 *Western Courier* hauling 3-CIG 1498 *Farringford* across the A351 road to Studland at Corfe Viaduct with a Swanage to Norden train. 7 May 2011.

Here we see Fastline-liveried 56301 (originally 56045) approaching Harman's Cross hauling 3-CIG 1498 *Farringford*, with the addition of an extra coach to boost capacity with a Norden to Swanage service. Unlikely as it seems, Class 56s were sometimes used to haul slam-door EMUs to try and maintain some sort of service at times of adverse weather during the 1970s and '80s, usually in the south-east where snowfall can sometimes be very disrupting. Nowadays, of course, trains are just simply cancelled at the occurrence of a few flakes! The Class 56 can still occasionally be seen working on the main line today and at the time of writing is on hire to Colas Rail. 8 May 2011.

Class 47s have inevitably appeared on the line from time to time and a popular visitor was main line-registered 'large logo' liveried 47580 *County of Essex*. The loco is seen here coming across Corfe Common with a Harman's Cross to Corfe Castle shuttle service, hauling 4-VEP 3417 *Gordon Pettitt* and with 33111 on the rear. 9 May 2010.

A few years later, it was the turn of 47292 in an unusual form of 'large logo' livery to appear, and in this shot is hauling the teak-liveried LUL 4-TC around Corfe Castle's approach curve on a Swanage to Norden service. This loco is currently on a five-year loan to the Churnet Valley Railway. 9 May 2014.

At the time of writing, the latest Class 47 to visit the line is the sole Freightliner-operated 47830 *Beechings Legacy*, which is seen departing from Harman's Cross hauling the now red-liveried LUL 4-TC on a Norden to Swanage service. This 47 is now only used very occasionally for a few stock moves or route-learning runs on the national network. 12 May 2023.

The only time I think the LUL 4-TC was used in push-pull mode during the 2023 gala was here as it approaches the Harman's Cross stop with a Norden to Swanage service, being propelled by 33111. The 98 headcode is correct for this line back in BR days. 12 May 2023.

Back in 2011, 3-CIG 1498 *Farringford* is being propelled across Corfe Common, about to pass beneath Townsend bridge by 33103 *Swordfish* whilst working a Norden to Swanage service. Again, this was not actually at a diesel gala but was one of the timetabled services on the line at the time. The unit actually proved to be quite handy working with the 33/1, as it saved many minutes' running the loco round at each end of the line. 8 June 2011.

On that same day in June 2011, this is 3-CIG 1498 *Farringford* once again being propelled by 33103 *Swordfish* soon after departing Corfe Castle with another Norden to Swanage service. This foot crossing just south of the station is a great place to see locos departing the station at Corfe Castle and working hard up a short incline towards Harman's Cross. 8 June 2011.

There are plenty of 'window hangers' here as 37521 *English China Clays* hauls 4-VEP 3417 *Gordon Pettitt* away from Harman's Cross with a train for Swanage. This battered-looking loco went on to have an interesting career after this gala. It first moved to Colas Rail and could be seen working test trains all over the national network, wearing this company's distinctive yellow and black livery, but after a few years it was deemed surplus and was then taken on by Locomotive Services Ltd (LSL), regaining BR green livery. It now often works various charter trains and stock moves around the country. 11 May 2013.

Loco Hauled/Propelled

At the same gala as in the previous shot, 4-VEP 3417 *Gordon Pettitt* is approaching Harman's Cross, propelled by both 33111+33108 on a Norden to Swanage service. It is showing headcode 97 for the Lymington branch this time! 11 May 2013.

This is the fine view of a southbound train arriving at Corfe Castle on a clear morning. 4-VEP 3417 *Gordon Pettitt* is being propelled by 33111 on a Norden to Swanage train, and is now displaying the correct headcode once again. In my opinion, there is no better view from any heritage line station than this. 9 May 2013.

This time, 4-VEP 3417 *Gordon Pettitt* is behind 33111 as they approach their destination at Norden with an arrival from Swanage. 9 May 2013.

Although this is a grey November morning, the footbridge at Corfe Castle also offers a superb view of southbound trains. 3-CIG 1498 *Farringford* is propelled into the station by 33111 on a Norden to Swanage train. This was on another non-gala day as can be judged by the total lack of people on the down platform. However, even for this time of year, that was quite unusual. 19 November 2011.

Later that same day, things brightened up markedly. 3-CIG 1498 *Farringford*, again being propelled by 33111, is this time on the approach to Harman's Cross. As can be seen by the plaque above its lower door, the signal box was built as recently as 1996. In BR days, there was neither a station nor a signal box at this location, just a single-track line. 19 November 2011.

The last view of this Swanage Railway series sees 3-CIG 1498 *Farringford* being propelled away from Norden by 33111 on another Norden to Swanage train. This is probably one of the most popular locations for photographers visiting the line, being just a short walking distance from either Corfe Castle station or Norden station. 19 November 2011.

To finish this volume, I have included a few odds and ends and something for the future. As mentioned earlier in this section, when older slam-door units were withdrawn in the past, some would see further service with engineers' departments for either test trains or for other reasons. During the late 1990s and early 2000s, Railtrack (now Network Rail) took on this unit, among others, and renumbered it 930206, under which identity it is seen working as a sandite/de-icer train at Tonbridge station. This was a former Class 416 2-EPB unit. Surprisingly, I think it is still intact today but am unsure where it is exactly. 13 November 2003.

For some years, 4-VEP 3417 *Gordon Pettitt* was stored under cover at Eastleigh Works where quite a bit of work and upkeep was undertaken. It is seen here during an arranged visit. 20 February 2009.

These two shots are certainly out of the ordinary! Way back in 1857, a branch line from Maiden Newton in Dorset to Bridport was opened and operated by the GWR. This line was extended in the mid-1880s to West Bay on the West Dorset coast, the GWR hoping that it would generate holiday traffic akin to places like Bournemouth and Weymouth, but that never really happened and this extension was closed in 1930. Freight traffic carried on until 1962, after which the extension was lifted. Remarkably, the station buildings at West Bay were left standing. They were derelict for many years but, now situated in the middle of a boatyard, were used as a glorified store room. By the late 1990s, the building was almost falling down by itself but, luckily, the council bought it and it was restored as a café. After many more years, even this facility has enjoyed a couple of changes in ownership. However, the latest owners have recognised the heritage of the building as a former railway station and, as a way to grow custom on the small site, have brought in former railway coaches to provide extended seating areas for diners. This is where our connection with slammers comes in; the first two coaches to arrive were No 70531, originally from a 4-CEP, but later from 4-CIG 'Greyhound' unit 1396; plus No 70292 from former 4-CEP 1554, later from 4-CIG 'Greyhound unit 1398. Ironically, these were placed on a length of track that has been relaid in the platform and as such is the only part of the former Bridport branch that has any track in place, so, from becoming the first to have track removed 60-odd-years ago it was the first to gain some back! This image shows the position of 70531 and 70292 as they were at this time. 10 January 2007.

This shot shows the delightful little station building dating from 1884 and the coaches mentioned in the previous shot. Since my visit here in 2007, the café has changed hands again and these two coaches have now moved north to Scotland, of all places. I have not yet sampled the dining here, but I am sure I will at some point. Judging by pictures I have seen, it looks even more inviting, and there are now a couple of different coaches in place. 10 January 2007.

One of the other significant preservation projects concerning slammers is the Swanage 4-TC Preservation Group's gradual restoration of unit 413 (in reality, coaches from other units) for eventual use on the Swanage Railway, and, maybe in the future, the main line, working with the line's Class 33111. In an advanced state of restoration in a siding at the rear of Corfe Castle station is driving coach 76275. 8 June 2019.

Just to bring things bang up to date in early 2024, 73109 *Battle of Britain – 80th Anniversary* has just arrived at the buffer stops at London Waterloo's platform 19, hauling 4-VEP 3417 *Gordon Pettitt* as 5Z73, the 10.42 Strawberry Hill C.S.D. to London Waterloo. This is the first slam-door EMU to be seen at London Waterloo since withdrawal back in the mid-2000s, running as part of Gordon Pettitt's birthday celebrations. 27 January 2024.

And finally, looking every bit a main line runner, 4-VEP 3417 *Gordon Pettitt* stands proudly at London Waterloo awaiting the arrival of Gordon Pettitt himself, who was brought up from Woking on a specially chartered Class 450 'Desiro' unit. Let's hope it is not long now before we see a slammer back on the main line. 27 January 2024.

Other books you might like:

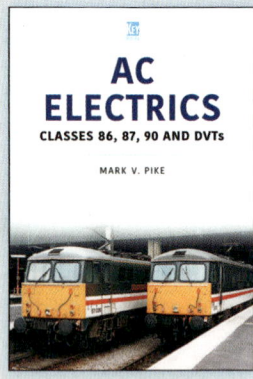

AC ELECTRICS
CLASSES 86, 87, 90 AND DVTs
MARK V. PIKE
Britain's Railways Series, Vol. 59

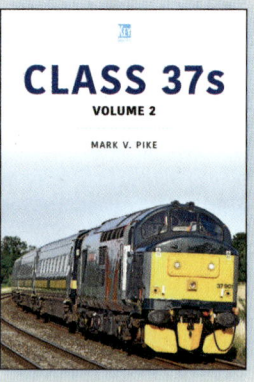

CLASS 37s
VOLUME 2
MARK V. PIKE
Britain's Railways Series, Vol. 55

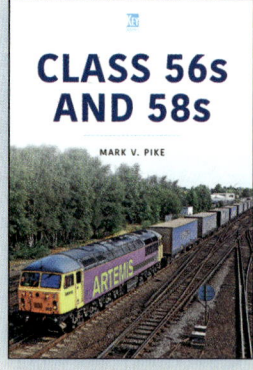

CLASS 56s AND 58s
MARK V. PIKE
Britain's Railways Series, Vol. 54

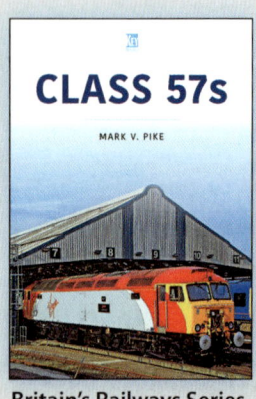

CLASS 57s
MARK V. PIKE
Britain's Railways Series, Vol. 53

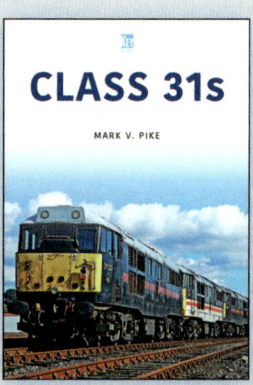

CLASS 31s
MARK V. PIKE
Britain's Railways Series, Vol. 50

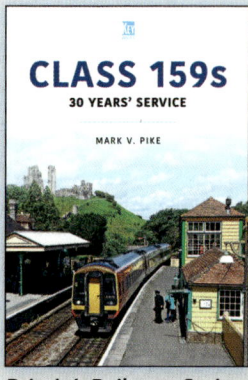

CLASS 159s
30 YEARS' SERVICE
MARK V. PIKE
Britain's Railways Series, Vol. 47

For our full range of titles please visit:
shop.keypublishing.com/books

VIP Book Club

Sign up today and receive
TWO FREE E-BOOKS

Be the first to find out about our forthcoming book releases and receive exclusive offers.

Register now at **keypublishing.com/vip-book-club**

Our VIP Book Club is a 100% spam-free zone, and we will never share your email with anyone else. You can read our full privacy policy at: privacy.keypublishing.com